CAMBRIDGE
UNIVERSITY PRESS

CAMBRIDGE
Global English Starters

Learner's Book C

Kathryn Harper & Gabrielle Pritchard

Welcome!

Cambridge Global English is a ten-stage course for learners of English as a Second Language (ESL). The ten stages range from the beginning of primary (Starters–Stage 6) to the end of lower secondary (Stages 7–9). It is ideal for all international ESL learners, and particularly for those following the Cambridge Primary and Lower Secondary English as a Second Language Curriculum Frameworks, as it has been written to adhere to these frameworks.

In addition to Learner's Book C, Cambridge Global English Starters Activity Book C provides supplementary support and practice. Cambridge Global English Starters Fun with Letters and Sounds C offers intensive practice in reading and writing of the upper- and lower-case letters learnt in lesson 4a of each unit. Comprehensive support for teachers is available in the Cambridge Global English Starters Teacher's Resource.

The following icons are used in this Learner's Book:

 Audio track number reference

 Differentiation

 Personalisation

 Critical thinking

For further explanation please refer to the teacher's resource.

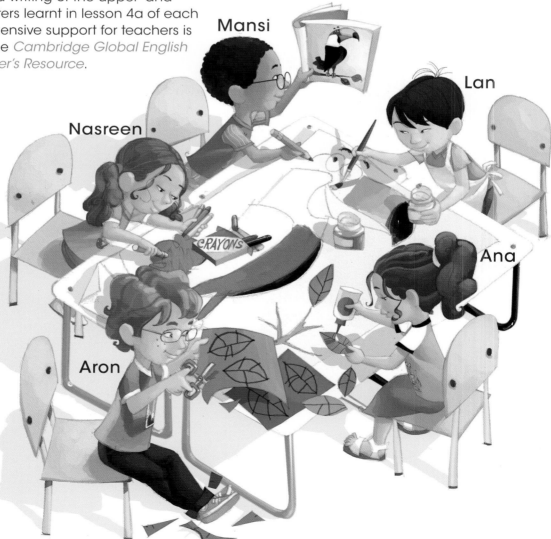

Mansi

Lan

Nasreen

Ana

Aron

Contents

Please see the teacher's resource for complete scope and sequence.

7 Homes!

1 Chant and clap.

Is it in the bedroom or bathroom?
Is it in the living room or kitchen?
Where's the teeny, tiny mouse
... hiding in our house?

2 What can you see? Explore.

Unit 7 Lesson 1 Words: bedroom, bathroom, living room, kitchen, flat, house Language: This is my (bedroom) Speaking: talk about the big picture, game
Listen and respond: chant, stick, say

 **3** 💭 ⇕ **Listen, find and say.**
Listen again and stick.

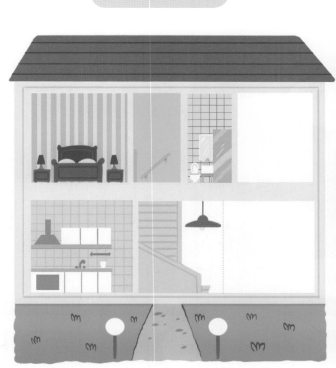

kitchen   living room   bathroom   bedroom

4 ⇕ **Play the game.**
Think of a room. Mime. Your friends guess the room.

2 Story time

Our wonderful home

🎧 **3** **1** ↕ **Listen and follow the story.**
Find the rooms in the story.

1 Look! This is our new house.

It's **not** a house.

2 It's a tree!

Yes, it is. It's a tree house. Come inside.

Whee! I love this house. It's fun.

3 This is the living room.

Ouch! This sofa is very, very hard.

4 I don't like it!

Unit 7 Lesson 2 words: tree, sofa, table, cooker, stairs, shower, bath, toy box, pet, inside, outside **Language:** There's a (cooker) in the (kitchen). There are (four) chairs)
Listen/Read: story **Speaking:** acting out story, sharing

Unit 7 Lesson 2 words: tree, sofa, table, cooker, stairs, shower, bath, toy box, pet, inside, outside **Language:** There's a (cooker) in the (kitchen). There are (four) chairs)
Listen/Read: story Speaking: acting out story, sharing

2a What kind of house do the family live in?

2b Which room is outside?

2c What unusual homes do you know about?

3 Look at the story. Play a game.

There's a brown toy box.

It's in a bedroom.

There are 2 green sofas.

They are in the living room.

4 Who doesn't like the new home?
Why? Why does she change her mind?

5 Values
Why is it important to share things?

1a What's coming out of the plane?
Look and say.

🎧 4 **1b** Listen and match.

2 Choose a room in your house.
Play.

Song: Welcome to my animal home

Chorus:
Welcome to my animal home
Where you are never, ever alone.
On the door, knock, knock, knock,
Turn the key, open the lock.

In the bedroom,
On the little red bed,
There's a funny brown rabbit
Bouncing on his head.
Boing, boing, boing.

In the kitchen,
Sitting on the chairs,
There are 2 big
Hungry black bears.
Grrrr.

In the bathroom,
Can you hear them laugh?
There are 3 white geese
Splashing in the bath.
Honk! Honk! Honk!

In the living room,
Sinking in the sofa deep,
There are 4 orange kittens
Oh, so fast asleep.
Shhhhhh.

4a Let's learn our ABC

 **1a** Listen, point and say.

 **1b** Listen, find and trace.

s un

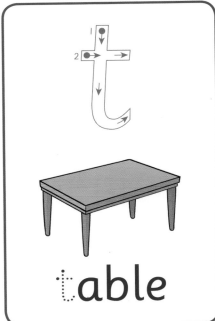

t able

u mbrella

2a 💭 Say and write the missing letters.

s quare   _ired   _mell   _ree   _ad   _riangle

 **2b** Listen and check.

2c 💭 Which letter is missing?

Say, join and check. Then write.

_mbrella

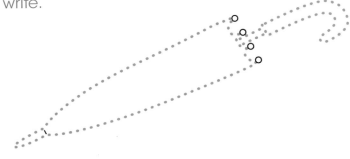

Unit 7 Lesson 4 Letters/sounds: s, t, u Words: sun, table, umbrella Numbers: 9, 10 Listen/say: alphabet words, number song

1 Look and say.

Write the numbers.

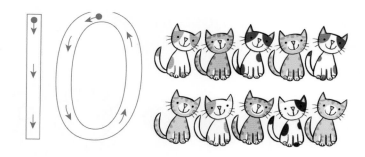

 **2a Listen and sing.**

We can count up, up, up
We can count up to 10.
1, 2, 3, 4, 5,
6, 7, 8, 9, 10.

We can count down, down, down
We can count down again.
10, 9, 8, 7, 6,
5, 4, 3, 2, 1.

We can count up to 10,
And we can count down again.
H-o-o-r-a-y!

2b Count and write.

1a 💭 What is a pattern?

1b Look at these things.

How are they patterns?

colours

big and small   shapes

1c 💭 Look at these patterns.

What kind are they? Tick ✓.

1

☐ colour
☐ big and small
☐ shapes

2

☐ colour
☐ big and small
☐ shapes

3

☐ colour
☐ big and small
☐ shapes

4

☐ colour
☐ big and small
☐ shapes

5

☐ colour
☐ big and small
☐ shapes

1d 🗨 Find the patterns in the room.

2a Explore your classroom.
Can you find patterns?
Draw or take pictures.

2b Show your patterns to the class.

Reflection 🗨
Which things create patterns
in more than 1 way?

6 Our project

1 Design your own tree house.
Work with a friend.

Choose a picture. Plan the rooms.

2 Make your tree house picture.

playroom

Complete your picture. Write the names of the rooms.

3 Tell the class about your tree house.

L👀k what I can do!

I can:

- 😊 talk about homes
- 😊 follow and understand a story
- 😊 talk about what is in my house
- 😊 identify and say the letters and sounds **s**, **t**, **u**
- 😊 count to 10
- 😊 describe patterns

1 Think about it What clothes make you feel good?

11 **1** ↕ Chant and clap.

A T-shirt, skirt and scarf,
A jumper, trousers and hat.
How do we pack all that?

2 💬 What can you see?
Explore the picture.

Unit 8 Lesson 1 Words: t-shirt, jumper, trousers, skirt, scarf, hat **Language:** He's/She's wearing a (yellow T-shirt) **Speaking:** talk about the big picture, game
Listen and respond: chant, stick, say

 **3** 🗨️ ⬆️⬇️ **Listen and stick.**
Then talk about the puppets.

scarf

hat

T-shirt   trousers   skirt   jumper

4 Play the clothes game.
Make 2 teams. Race to find the right clothes.

Find an orange and white scarf.

What's Granny making?

🎧 13 **1** ↕ **Listen and follow the story.**
Look at the first picture. What is Granny making?

Unit 8 Lesson 2 Words: Granny, long, short wear winter, warm **Listen/Read:** story **Speaking:** acting out story, taking care of your family

Unit 8 Lesson 2 Words: Granny, long, short wear winter, warm **Listen/Read:** story **Speaking:** acting out story, taking care of your family

2 💭 Who is it?
Match and say.

3 Trace to match the clothes to the characters.

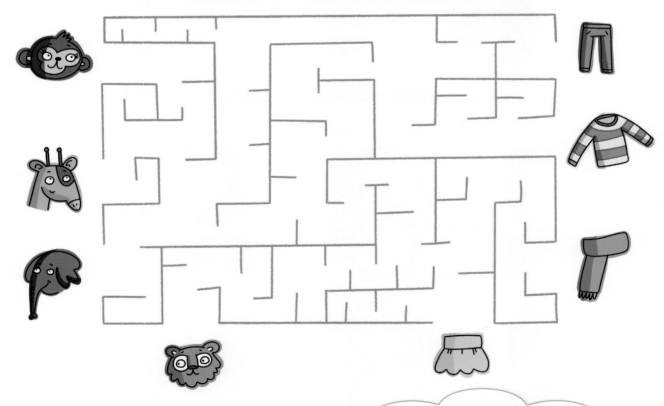

4 💭 Why do the animals want. new clothes?

 5 Listen and act out the story.

6 Values
How can you take care
of your family?

23

3 Talk about it   He's wearing a ...

1a What's missing? Say and stick.

 **1b** Listen and say 'yes' or 'no'.

1c Say what the boy and girl are wearing.

1d What's the weather like for the girl and boy?

2a 💭 Look at the children's clothes and guess what the weather is like.
Circle and say.

2b What's the weather like today?
What are your friends wearing?

Unit 8 Lesson 3 Words: windy, rainy, sunny, sunglasses, jacket **Language:** He/she's wearing (a hat). What's the weather like? It's (sunny) today. **Listen/say:** game, song

Stickers for Unit 7 page 5

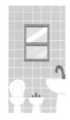

Stickers for Unit 8 page 19

Stickers for Unit 8 page 24

Stickers for Unit 9 page 33

Stickers for Unit 9 page 38

 **3 Match to the verses.**

Then listen, sing and act out.

Song: Can I go out to play?

Please, please Mum,
Can I go out to play?
I don't know …
It's cold today.
I'm wearing a hat.
Am I allowed to play?
Well. OK!

Please, please Mum,
Can I go out to play?
I don't know …
It's windy today.
I'm wearing a jumper.
Am I allowed to play?
Well. OK!

Please, please Mum,
Can I go out to play?
I don't know …
It's sunny today.
I'm wearing sunglasses.
Am I allowed to play?
Well. OK!

Please, please Mum,
Can I go out to play?
I don't know …
It's rainy today.
I'm wearing a jacket.
Am I allowed to play?
Well. OK!

 **1a** Listen, point and say.

violin

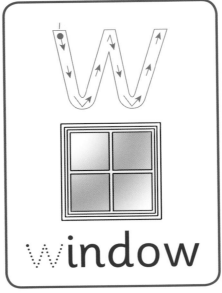

window

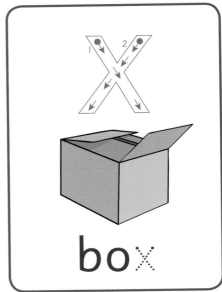

box

 **1b** Listen, find and trace.

 **2a** 💭 Talk about the pictures.
Then listen, point and say.

orm   fo   _ase

toy bo_   _an   _olf

 **2b** Listen and write the missing letters.

1 How many?

Write the numbers.

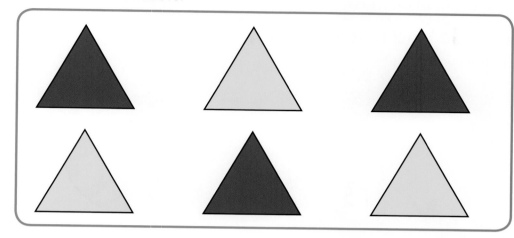

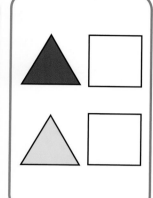

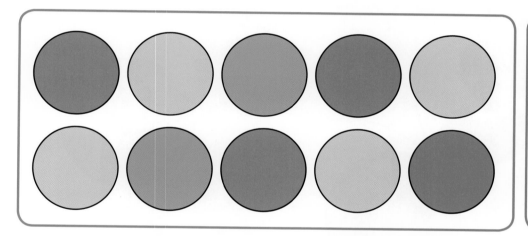

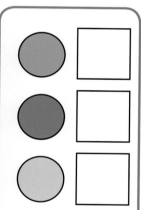

2 Add and write the answer.

(1)  ___ + ___ = ☐

(2) ___ + ___ = ☐

(3) ___ + ___ = ☐

(4) ___ + ___ = ☐

5 Find out more   The clothes we wear each day

1a 💭 **Think about your day.**
When do you wear different clothes?

🎧 21 **1b** 💭 **Listen and trace and follow the day.**
What are the children wearing?

Unit 8 Lesson 5 CLIL Social Studies **Words:** football, dancing, pyjamas, bib dinner time, School time **Listen/say:** talk about clothes and daily routines

2a What are you wearing? Draw and colour.

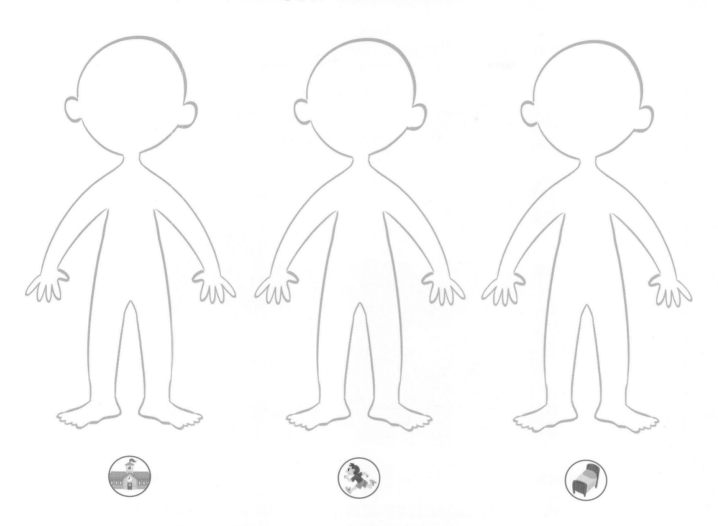

2b It's daytime and you're not at school.
What are you wearing?
Draw and tell the class.

Reflection

Why are some clothes
good for playing in?

6 Our project

1 Design and make clothes.

2 Make a display.

Lana   Ali   Enid

3 Talk about your doll.

Luiz   Lana   Ali   Enid

My doll is wearing blue trousers and a green shirt.

L👀k what I can do!

I can:

- 🙂 talk about which clothes make us feel good
- 🙂 talk about clothes
- 🙂 follow and understand a story
- 🙂 understand why we wear different clothes
- 🙂 identify and say the letters and sounds **v**, **w**, **x**
- 🙂 count to 10 and add numbers

9 In my garden

1 Think about it What can we find in the garden?

22 **1** ⇕ Chant and clap.

On a plant near the pond,
I see a spider, bird and bee,
And a little ladybird climbing a tree.

2 💭 What can you see?
Explore the picture.

Unit 9 Lesson 1 Words: plant, pond, spider, bird, bee, ladybird, butterfly **Speaking:** talk about the big picture, game **Listen and respond:** chant, stick, say

 **3**  **Listen and stick.**
Then talk about the picture.

plant   bee   bird

1   5   4   6

3   2

ladybird   spider   butterfly

4 Play the bug game.
Choose a leader. Tell your bugs what to do.

Ladybirds, ladybirds fly away.

Ladybirds, ladybirds come home again.

2 Story time

Jack and the beanstalk

24 **1a** ⇅ **Listen and follow the story.**

Look at the pictures on this page. What does the beanstalk come from?

1b Can you find 4 little bugs in the story?

1 Jack and his mum are poor.

Mum.
Cow is hungry.

There is no food.
Take Cow to market.

Moo!

2 A man sees Jack.

Can I buy your cow?

OK.

The man gives Jack 6 beans.

3 Mum is angry.

The beans are no good.

She throws the beans in the garden.

4 The next day.

Where are the beans?

Look!
There's a **giant** plant.
It's a beanstalk!

5 Jack climbs up.

Where are you going?

I'm going **up**, **up**, **up**.

6

Next to the beanstalk is a **giant** house. Jack goes inside.

7 He sees a gold bird on the table.

Fee-fi-fo-fum. I smell a small boy! Where are you?

8

Oh no! It's a big, big giant!

Jack hides under the table.

9

Give me a gold egg, bird!

10 Jack jumps out.

This gold egg is for me!

11 Jack climbs down.

Where are you going, boy? I'm **hungry**!

I'm going down, down, down.

12

Look. We've got a big egg!

It's gold! Good boy, Jack!

Unit 9 Lesson 2 **words:** cow, hungry, market, beans, giant, beanstalk, up, down **Listen/Read:** story **Speaking:** acting out story, being safe

2 Look, choose and trace.

Mum man

Giant Jack

beanstalk beans

bird egg

up down

3a Why does Mum like the egg?

3b What will Mum and Jack do with the egg?

4 Make a big beanstalk.

5 Listen and act out the story.

6 Values
How can we be safe?

3 Talk about it Where are they?

26 **1a** Listen, point and say.

1b ⇅ Where's the bee? Read and match.

in   next to   on   under

27 **2** Where are they?
Listen and stick. Then say.

The bird is in the house.

Unit 9 Lesson 3 **Words:** in, next to, on, under, flower, garden, knee **Language:** The bird is (in) the house. **Listen/say:** gome, song

3a Look and match.

Then listen and sing.

Song: In my garden

In my garden, I can see
A purple butterfly
Under the tree.
I'm looking round my garden,
Looking round my garden.

In my garden, I can hear
A buzzing bee
Next to my ear …
I'm looking round my garden,
Looking round my garden.

In my garden, I can see
A yellow bird
In the tree …
I'm looking round my garden,
Looking round my garden.

In my garden, I can see
A big, black spider
On my knee.
EEEE!
I'm running out of my garden,
Running out of my garden!

3b Listen and draw.

Then listen, sing and act out.

 **1a** Listen, point and say.

yellow

zoo

 **1b** Listen, find and trace.

2a Look and guess.
Then join the dots.

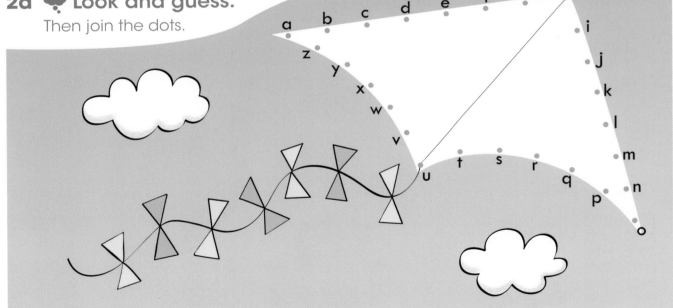

2b Complete the sentence, then colour.

It's a __ellow __ __ __ __.

 **3** Listen and do the alphabet rap.

1 How many animals?

Write the numbers.

2 How many?

Write the numbers.

① 🐟 🐟 🐟 + 🐟 🐟 = [5]

② 🐝 🐝 + 🐝 🐝 = [ ]

③ + = [ ]

④ 🐱 🐱 🐱 + 🐱 🐱 🐱 = [ ]

⑤ + = [ ]

1a  What comes from eggs?
Match.

egg

no egg

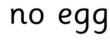

1b Talk about the animals.

Birds come from eggs.

2a 💭 Find the eggs in the picture.

2b 💭 Match the animals to the eggs.

2c 💭 Say where the eggs are found.

The frog eggs are on the ...

fish

frog

bird

butterfly

spider

Reflection

What is similar about animals that come from eggs?

43

6 Our project

1 Go on a minibeast hunt.
Do a minibeast survey outside.

2 Make a class graph.
Put the minibeasts on the graph.

3 💭 **Talk about your results.**

There are 3 bees.

Look what I can do!

I can:

- 😊 talk about what we can find in the garden
- 😊 follow and understand a story
- 😊 talk about where things are
- 😊 identify and say the letters and sounds **y**, **z**
- 😊 say and write the alphabet
- 😊 add 1, 2 or 3
- 😊 talk about what comes from eggs
- 😊 talk about minibeasts/small animals

What can we remember?

 **1** Listen and draw lines.

2 Listen and say.

Then trace or tick ✓ the correct answer.

1	☐ bedroom	☐ bathroom	☐ living room
2	☐ bathroom	☐ living room	☐ garden
3	☐ kitchen	☐ bedroom	☐ living room
4	☐ bathroom	☐ bedroom	☐ kitchen
5	☐ garden	☐ kitchen	☐ living room
6	☐ bedroom	☐ living room	☐ bathroom

47

3 Listen and tick ✓ the box.

1

a ☐   b ☐   c ☐

2

a ☐   b ☐   c ☐

3

a ☐   b ☐   c ☐

4

a ☐   b ☐   c ☐

5

a ☐   b ☐   c ☐